Adulting With Loans

Adulting With Loans

Don't think of it
like a burden.
Think of it as a
a challenge
you've already
conquered.

Adulting With Loans

36 Month Budget Tracker,
Repayment Guide & Emergency
Fund Builder for Grads

Welcome, Graduate!

You Did It!

Congratulations—you made it.

You walked across that stage (or logged in for a virtual ceremony), tossed your cap, and officially joined the ranks of college graduates. That's no small feat. Whether your journey was smooth or full of detours, you showed up, kept going, and earned this moment.

Now, as you step into your next chapter, there's one thing you might be carrying with you: **student loan debt**. And that's okay.

Over **43 million Americans** have student loans. You're not alone—and more importantly, you're not "failing." You invested in your future. Now, this planner is here to help you take back control, one smart decision at a time.

This isn't just a debt tracker.

It's your roadmap to freedom, clarity, and confidence.

Let's begin.

Your Debt Doesn't Define You

It's easy to feel like your loans are a shadow following you everywhere—into job interviews, apartment leases, even coffee dates. But here's the truth:

Your debt is a financial circumstance—not your worth.

You are not "bad with money" because you borrowed to get an education.

You are not "behind" because you're still paying it off.

You are **strategic**, **resilient**, and **capable**—and this planner will help you prove it to yourself.

This journey isn't about punishment or deprivation.

It's about **intention**.

Every payment you make is a vote for your future self—the one who wakes up debt-free, breathing easier, and building the life you want.

So be kind to yourself. Progress > perfection.

How to Use This Planner

This isn't a test. There are no wrong answers—only honest ones.

Here's how to get the most out of this book:

Start where you are.

Don't wait until you "have your finances together." Begin today, with what you know.

✅ **Be consistent, not perfect.**
Missed a week? Forgot to log a payment? Just pick up where you left off. Momentum builds over time.

✅ **Track more than money.**
Notice how you feel as you pay down debt. Relief, pride, frustration—they're all valid. Jot them down. Your emotional journey matters too.

✅ **Celebrate every win.**
Paid $5 extra? Called your loan servicer? Said no to an impulse buy? That's victory. Write it down. Say it out loud.

This planner works best when you treat it like a conversation with your future self—one full of honesty, hope, and hustle.

Why Mindset Matters (More Than Math)

Yes, interest rates and repayment plans matter.

But **your mindset** determines whether you stick with it when things get tough.

Research shows that people who **track progress visually** and **connect payments to personal goals** pay off debt faster—even with the same income.

That's why this planner includes:

Visual payoff trackers (so you *see* your progress)

Space to define your "why" (freedom, travel, homeownership, peace of mind)

Prompts to reflect on wins (to fight burnout)

Remember:

Paying off student loans isn't just about money.

It's about **reclaiming your choices.**

Every dollar you send toward your loans is a brick in the foundation of your freedom.

Your First Step Starts Now

Before you turn the page, take 2 minutes to do this:

🖊 **Write your "Debt-Free Vision"**

What will your life look like when your loans are gone?

Examples:

"I'll finally start saving for a home."

"I'll sleep without that monthly dread."

"I'll feel proud telling my younger sibling I did it."

Write it below. Keep it visible. Come back to it when motivation dips.

My debt-free vision:

You've already done the hard part—showing up.

Now, let's build your way out, one page at a time.

Onward,

—Your Future Self (who's already thanking you)

You got this!

SWIPING WITH A SMILE.

Student Loan Inventory Worksheet

For Recent Graduates Managing Student Debt

Tip: Log in to StudentAid.gov to find details for all federal loans. For private loans, check your monthly statements or contact your lender.

Step 1: List Every Loan

#	Loan Name (e.g., Direct Unsubsi-dized)	Loan Type (Federal / Private)	Loan Servicer or Lender	Current Balance	Interest Rate (%)	Repayment Plan	Monthly Payment	Subsidized? (Y/N)	Grace Period End Date
1									
2									
3									
4									
5									
6									

Definitions

Subsidized: The government pays interest while you're in school (federal only).

Servicer: Company managing your federal loan (e.g., MOHELA, Nelnet).

Grace Period: Usually 6 months after graduation before repayment begins.

Step 2: Summary Totals

Total Federal Loan Debt: $ ____________________

Total Private Loan Debt: $ ____________________

Combined Total Debt: $ ____________________

Weighted Average Interest Rate: _____%
(Formula: $\sum(\text{Balance} \times \text{Rate}) / \text{Total Debt}$)

Step 3: Key Action Checklist

_ Verified all federal loans at StudentAid.gov
_ Know my first payment due date
_ Created accounts with all loan servicers
_ Researched income-driven repayment (IDR) options
_ Enrolled (or plan to enroll) in autopay for interest rate discount
_ Saved contact info for each lender/servicer

EMERGENCY
FUND
FUTURE SELF HIGH-FIVE!

Income & Expense Tracker

Your First Job, Your Financial Fresh Start

Hey there, grad!

Congratulations on landing your first real job—you've worked hard to get here! Now that your paycheck is rolling in, it's the perfect time to build simple money habits that will pay off *big time* in the future.

Tracking your income and expenses isn't about restriction—it's about **awareness**. When you know exactly where your money goes, you can:

Make your student loan payments without panic

Avoid living paycheck to paycheck

Save for fun things (yes, even weekend trips!)

Build confidence that you're in control of your life

Think of this tracker as your financial GPS. You don't need perfection—just honesty and a little consistency. Even 10 minutes a week can help you spot leaks, celebrate wins, and stay aligned with your goals.

And remember: **Every dollar you track is a step closer to freedom.**

Month ______________________________

Monthly Take-Home Pay (After Taxes)

$ ____________________

(This is your net income—the amount that actually hits your bank account.)

Fixed Expenses *(Same amount every month)*

Category	*Budgetd Amount*	*Actual Spent*
Rent	*$*	*$*
Utilities (electric, water, internet)	*$*	*$*
Phone Bill	*$*	*$*
Student Loan Payment	*$*	*$*
Transportation (car payment, gas, transit pass)	*$*	*$*
Insurance (health, car, renters)	*$*	*$*
Subscriptions (Spotify, Netflix, etc.)	*$*	*$*
Total Fixed	*$*	*$*

Variable Expenses (*Changes each month.*)

Category	*Budgeted Amount*	*Actual Spent*
Groceries	*$*	*$*
Dining Out / Coffee	*$*	*$*
Entertainment (movies, concerts, etc.)	*$*	*$*
Shopping (clothes, gadgets, etc.)	*$*	*$*
Personal Care (haircut, toiletries)	*$*	*$*
Side Hustle Costs (if applicable)	*$*	*$*
Gifts / Donations	*$*	*$*
Total Variable	$	$

Financial Goals this Month

Category	*Amount*
Emergency Fund Savings	*$*
Extra Student Loan Payment	*$*
Retirement (e.g., 401k or Roth IRA)	*$*
Fun Money Set Aside	*$*
Total Goals	*$*

Monthly Summary

Total Income: $ ____________________

Total Spent (Fixed + Variable): $ ______________

Amount Left Over: $ ____________

(Income – Total Spent = What you can save, invest, or roll into next month)

Reflection: Did you spend more than planned on dining out? That's okay! Awareness is the first step. Next month, maybe you pack lunch twice a week and redirect that $40 toward your loan. Small shifts create big results.

My Money Goal for This Month:

"This month, I will ____
because I'm building a future where I'm free from debt and full of possibility."

Your name: ____

Month: ____

Remember: ____

You're not just budgeting—**you're designing your life**. Every conscious choice today gives you more freedom tomorrow. Keep going—you've got this!

Month ____

Monthly Take-Home Pay (After Taxes)

$ ______________________

(This is your net income—the amount that actually hits your bank account.)

Fixed Expenses *(Same amount every month)*

Category	*Budgetd Amount*	*Actual Spent*
Rent	*$*	*$*
Utilities (electric, water, internet)	*$*	*$*
Phone Bill	*$*	*$*
Student Loan Payment	*$*	*$*
Transportation (car payment, gas, transit pass)	*$*	*$*
Insurance (health, car, renters)	*$*	*$*
Subscriptions (Spotify, Netflix, etc.)	*$*	*$*
Total Fixed	*$*	*$*

Variable Expenses (*Changes each month.*)

Category	*Budgeted Amount*	*Actual Spent*
Groceries	*$*	*$*
Dining Out / Coffee	*$*	*$*
Entertainment (movies, concerts, etc.)	*$*	*$*
Shopping (clothes, gadgets, etc.)	*$*	*$*
Personal Care (haircut, toiletries)	*$*	*$*
Side Hustle Costs (if applicable)	*$*	*$*
Gifts / Donations	*$*	*$*
Total Variable	$	$

Financial Goals this Month

Category	*Amount*
Emergency Fund Savings	*$*
Extra Student Loan Payment	*$*
Retirement (e.g., 401k or Roth IRA)	*$*
Fun Money Set Aside	*$*
Total Goals	*$*

Monthly Summary

Total Income: $ ______________________

Total Spent (Fixed + Variable): $ ________________

Amount Left Over: $ _____________

(Income – Total Spent = What you can save, invest, or roll into next month)

Reflection: Did you spend more than planned on dining out? That's okay! Awareness is the first step. Next month, maybe you pack lunch twice a week and redirect that $40 toward your loan. Small shifts create big results.

My Money Goal for This Month:

"This month, I will ____
because I'm building a future where I'm free from debt and full of possibility."

Your name: ____

Month: ____

Remember: ____

You're not just budgeting—**you're designing your life**. Every conscious choice today gives you more freedom tomorrow. Keep going—you've got this!

Month ________________________________

Monthly Take-Home Pay (After Taxes)

$ ____________________

(This is your net income—the amount that actually hits your bank account.)

Fixed Expenses *(Same amount every month)*

Category	*Budgetd Amount*	*Actual Spent*
Rent	$	$
Utilities (electric, water, internet)	$	$
Phone Bill	$	$
Student Loan Payment	$	$
Transportation (car payment, gas, transit pass)	$	$
Insurance (health, car, renters)	$	$
Subscriptions (Spotify, Netflix, etc.)	$	$
Total Fixed	$	$

Variable Expenses (*Changes each month.*)

Category	*Budgeted Amount*	*Actual Spent*
Groceries	$	$
Dining Out / Coffee	$	$
Entertainment (movies, concerts, etc.)	$	$
Shopping (clothes, gadgets, etc.)	$	$
Personal Care (haircut, toiletries)	$	$
Side Hustle Costs (if applicable)	$	$
Gifts / Donations	$	$
Total Variable	$	$

Financial Goals this Month

Category	*Amount*
Emergency Fund Savings	*$*
Extra Student Loan Payment	*$*
Retirement (e.g., 401k or Roth IRA)	*$*
Fun Money Set Aside	*$*
Total Goals	*$*

Monthly Summary

Total Income: $ ____________________

Total Spent (Fixed + Variable): $ ______________

Amount Left Over: $ ___________

(Income – Total Spent = What you can save, invest, or roll into next month)

Reflection: Did you spend more than planned on dining out? That's okay! Awareness is the first step. Next month, maybe you pack lunch twice a week and redirect that $40 toward your loan. Small shifts create big results.

My Money Goal for This Month:

"This month, I will____
because I'm building a future where I'm free from debt and full of possibility."

Your name: ____

Month: ____

Remember: ____

You're not just budgeting—**you're designing your life**. Every conscious choice today gives you more freedom tomorrow. Keep going—you've got this!

Month ______________________________

Monthly Take-Home Pay (After Taxes)

$ ________________

(This is your net income—the amount that actually hits your bank account.)

Fixed Expenses *(Same amount every month)*

Category	*Budgetd Amount*	*Actual Spent*
Rent	$	$
Utilities (electric, water, internet)	$	$
Phone Bill	$	$
Student Loan Payment	$	$
Transportation (car payment, gas, transit pass)	$	$
Insurance (health, car, renters)	$	$
Subscriptions (Spotify, Netflix, etc.)	$	$
Total Fixed	$	$

Variable Expenses (*Changes each month.*)

Category	*Budgeted Amount*	*Actual Spent*
Groceries	$	$
Dining Out / Coffee	$	$
Entertainment (movies, concerts, etc.)	$	$
Shopping (clothes, gadgets, etc.)	$	$
Personal Care (haircut, toiletries)	$	$
Side Hustle Costs (if applicable)	$	$
Gifts / Donations	$	$
Total Variable	$	$

Financial Goals this Month

Category	*Amount*
Emergency Fund Savings	*$*
Extra Student Loan Payment	*$*
Retirement (e.g., 401k or Roth IRA)	*$*
Fun Money Set Aside	*$*
Total Goals	*$*

Monthly Summary

Total Income: $ ______________________

Total Spent (Fixed + Variable): $ ________________

Amount Left Over: $ _____________

(Income – Total Spent = What you can save, invest, or roll into next month)

Reflection: Did you spend more than planned on dining out? That's okay! Awareness is the first step. Next month, maybe you pack lunch twice a week and redirect that $40 toward your loan. Small shifts create big results.

My Money Goal for This Month:

"This month, I will ____
because I'm building a future where I'm free from debt and full of possibility."

Your name: ____

Month: ____

Remember: ____

You're not just budgeting—**you're designing your life**. Every conscious choice today gives you more freedom tomorrow. Keep going—you've got this!

Month ______________________________

Monthly Take-Home Pay (After Taxes)

$ ______________________

(This is your net income—the amount that actually hits your bank account.)

Fixed Expenses *(Same amount every month)*

Category	*Budgetd Amount*	*Actual Spent*
Rent	*$*	*$*
Utilities (electric, water, internet)	*$*	*$*
Phone Bill	*$*	*$*
Student Loan Payment	*$*	*$*
Transportation (car payment, gas, transit pass)	*$*	*$*
Insurance (health, car, renters)	*$*	*$*
Subscriptions (Spotify, Netflix, etc.)	*$*	*$*
Total Fixed	*$*	*$*

Variable Expenses (*Changes each month.*)

Category	*Budgeted Amount*	*Actual Spent*
Groceries	*$*	*$*
Dining Out / Coffee	*$*	*$*
Entertainment (movies, concerts, etc.)	*$*	*$*
Shopping (clothes, gadgets, etc.)	*$*	*$*
Personal Care (haircut, toiletries)	*$*	*$*
Side Hustle Costs (if applicable)	*$*	*$*
Gifts / Donations	*$*	*$*
Total Variable	$	$

Financial Goals this Month

Category	*Amount*
Emergency Fund Savings	*$*
Extra Student Loan Payment	*$*
Retirement (e.g., 401k or Roth IRA)	*$*
Fun Money Set Aside	*$*
Total Goals	*$*

Monthly Summary

Total Income: $ ______________________

Total Spent (Fixed + Variable): $ ________________

Amount Left Over: $ ____________

(Income – Total Spent = What you can save, invest, or roll into next month)

Reflection: Did you spend more than planned on dining out? That's okay! Awareness is the first step. Next month, maybe you pack lunch twice a week and redirect that $40 toward your loan. Small shifts create big results.

My Money Goal for This Month:

"This month, I will____
because I'm building a future where I'm free from debt and full of possibility."

Your name: ____

Month: ____

Remember: ____

You're not just budgeting—**you're designing your life**. Every conscious choice today gives you more freedom tomorrow. Keep going—you've got this!

Month ______________________________

Monthly Take-Home Pay (After Taxes)

$ ____________________

(This is your net income—the amount that actually hits your bank account.)

Fixed Expenses *(Same amount every month)*

Category	*Budgetd Amount*	*Actual Spent*
Rent	*$*	*$*
Utilities (electric, water, internet)	*$*	*$*
Phone Bill	*$*	*$*
Student Loan Payment	*$*	*$*
Transportation (car payment, gas, transit pass)	*$*	*$*
Insurance (health, car, renters)	*$*	*$*
Subscriptions (Spotify, Netflix, etc.)	*$*	*$*
Total Fixed	*$*	*$*

Variable Expenses (*Changes each month.*)

Category	*Budgeted Amount*	*Actual Spent*
Groceries	*$*	*$*
Dining Out / Coffee	*$*	*$*
Entertainment (movies, concerts, etc.)	*$*	*$*
Shopping (clothes, gadgets, etc.)	*$*	*$*
Personal Care (haircut, toiletries)	*$*	*$*
Side Hustle Costs (if applicable)	*$*	*$*
Gifts / Donations	*$*	*$*
Total Variable	$	$

Financial Goals this Month

Category	*Amount*
Emergency Fund Savings	*$*
Extra Student Loan Payment	*$*
Retirement (e.g., 401k or Roth IRA)	*$*
Fun Money Set Aside	*$*
Total Goals	*$*

Monthly Summary

Total Income: $ ______________________

Total Spent (Fixed + Variable): $ ________________

Amount Left Over: $ _____________

(Income – Total Spent = What you can save, invest, or roll into next month)

Reflection: Did you spend more than planned on dining out? That's okay! Awareness is the first step. Next month, maybe you pack lunch twice a week and redirect that $40 toward your loan. Small shifts create big results.

My Money Goal for This Month:

"This month, I will ____
because I'm building a future where I'm free from debt and full of possibility."

Your name: ____

Month: ____

Remember: ____

You're not just budgeting—**you're designing your life**. Every conscious choice today gives you more freedom tomorrow. Keep going—you've got this!

Month ______________________________

Monthly Take-Home Pay (After Taxes)

$ ____________________

(This is your net income—the amount that actually hits your bank account.)

Fixed Expenses *(Same amount every month)*

Category	*Budgetd Amount*	*Actual Spent*
Rent	*$*	*$*
Utilities (electric, water, internet)	*$*	*$*
Phone Bill	*$*	*$*
Student Loan Payment	*$*	*$*
Transportation (car payment, gas, transit pass)	*$*	*$*
Insurance (health, car, renters)	*$*	*$*
Subscriptions (Spotify, Netflix, etc.)	*$*	*$*
Total Fixed	*$*	*$*

Variable Expenses (*Changes each month.*)

Category	*Budgeted Amount*	*Actual Spent*
Groceries	*$*	*$*
Dining Out / Coffee	*$*	*$*
Entertainment (movies, concerts, etc.)	*$*	*$*
Shopping (clothes, gadgets, etc.)	*$*	*$*
Personal Care (haircut, toiletries)	*$*	*$*
Side Hustle Costs (if applicable)	*$*	*$*
Gifts / Donations	*$*	*$*
Total Variable	$	$

Financial Goals this Month

Category	*Amount*
Emergency Fund Savings	*$*
Extra Student Loan Payment	*$*
Retirement (e.g., 401k or Roth IRA)	*$*
Fun Money Set Aside	*$*
Total Goals	*$*

Monthly Summary

Total Income: $ ________________________

Total Spent (Fixed + Variable): $ ________________

Amount Left Over: $ ______________

(Income – Total Spent = What you can save, invest, or roll into next month)

Reflection: Did you spend more than planned on dining out? That's okay! Awareness is the first step. Next month, maybe you pack lunch twice a week and redirect that $40 toward your loan. Small shifts create big results.

My Money Goal for This Month:

"This month, I will ____ *because I'm building a future where I'm free from debt and full of possibility."*

Your name: ____

Month: ____

Remember: ____

You're not just budgeting—**you're designing your life**. Every conscious choice today gives you more freedom tomorrow. Keep going—you've got this!

Month ______________________________

Monthly Take-Home Pay (After Taxes)

$ ____________________

(This is your net income—the amount that actually hits your bank account.)

Fixed Expenses *(Same amount every month)*

Category	*Budgetd Amount*	*Actual Spent*
Rent	$	$
Utilities (electric, water, internet)	$	$
Phone Bill	$	$
Student Loan Payment	$	$
Transportation (car payment, gas, transit pass)	$	$
Insurance (health, car, renters)	$	$
Subscriptions (Spotify, Netflix, etc.)	$	$
Total Fixed	$	$

Variable Expenses (*Changes each month.*)

Category	*Budgeted Amount*	*Actual Spent*
Groceries	$	$
Dining Out / Coffee	$	$
Entertainment (movies, concerts, etc.)	$	$
Shopping (clothes, gadgets, etc.)	$	$
Personal Care (haircut, toiletries)	$	$
Side Hustle Costs (if applicable)	$	$
Gifts / Donations	$	$
Total Variable	$	$

Financial Goals this Month

Category	*Amount*
Emergency Fund Savings	*$*
Extra Student Loan Payment	*$*
Retirement (e.g., 401k or Roth IRA)	*$*
Fun Money Set Aside	*$*
Total Goals	*$*

Monthly Summary

Total Income: $ ______________________

Total Spent (Fixed + Variable): $ ________________

Amount Left Over: $ _____________

(Income – Total Spent = What you can save, invest, or roll into next month)

Reflection: Did you spend more than planned on dining out? That's okay! Awareness is the first step. Next month, maybe you pack lunch twice a week and redirect that $40 toward your loan. Small shifts create big results.

My Money Goal for This Month:

"This month, I will____
because I'm building a future where I'm free from debt and full of possibility."

Your name: ____

Month: ____

Remember: ____

You're not just budgeting—**you're designing your life**. Every conscious choice today gives you more freedom tomorrow. Keep going—you've got this!

Month ____________________

Monthly Take-Home Pay (After Taxes)

$ ____________________

(This is your net income—the amount that actually hits your bank account.)

Fixed Expenses *(Same amount every month)*

Category	*Budgetd Amount*	*Actual Spent*
Rent	$	$
Utilities (electric, water, internet)	$	$
Phone Bill	$	$
Student Loan Payment	$	$
Transportation (car payment, gas, transit pass)	$	$
Insurance (health, car, renters)	$	$
Subscriptions (Spotify, Netflix, etc.)	$	$
Total Fixed	$	$

Variable Expenses (*Changes each month.*)

Category	*Budgeted Amount*	*Actual Spent*
Groceries	$	$
Dining Out / Coffee	$	$
Entertainment (movies, concerts, etc.)	$	$
Shopping (clothes, gadgets, etc.)	$	$
Personal Care (haircut, toiletries)	$	$
Side Hustle Costs (if applicable)	$	$
Gifts / Donations	$	$
Total Variable	$	$

Financial Goals this Month

Category	*Amount*
Emergency Fund Savings	*$*
Extra Student Loan Payment	*$*
Retirement (e.g., 401k or Roth IRA)	*$*
Fun Money Set Aside	*$*
Total Goals	*$*

Monthly Summary

Total Income: $ ____________________

Total Spent (Fixed + Variable): $ ______________

Amount Left Over: $ ____________

(Income – Total Spent = What you can save, invest, or roll into next month)

Reflection: Did you spend more than planned on dining out? That's okay! Awareness is the first step. Next month, maybe you pack lunch twice a week and redirect that $40 toward your loan. Small shifts create big results.

My Money Goal for This Month:

"This month, I will ____
because I'm building a future where I'm free from debt and full of possibility."

Your name: ____

Month: ____

Remember: ____

You're not just budgeting—**you're designing your life**. Every conscious choice today gives you more freedom tomorrow. Keep going—you've got this!

Month ________________________________

Monthly Take-Home Pay (After Taxes)

$ ____________________

(This is your net income—the amount that actually hits your bank account.)

Fixed Expenses *(Same amount every month)*

Category	*Budgetd Amount*	*Actual Spent*
Rent	*$*	*$*
Utilities (electric, water, internet)	*$*	*$*
Phone Bill	*$*	*$*
Student Loan Payment	*$*	*$*
Transportation (car payment, gas, transit pass)	*$*	*$*
Insurance (health, car, renters)	*$*	*$*
Subscriptions (Spotify, Netflix, etc.)	*$*	*$*
Total Fixed	*$*	*$*

Variable Expenses (*Changes each month.*)

Category	*Budgeted Amount*	*Actual Spent*
Groceries	*$*	*$*
Dining Out / Coffee	*$*	*$*
Entertainment (movies, concerts, etc.)	*$*	*$*
Shopping (clothes, gadgets, etc.)	*$*	*$*
Personal Care (haircut, toiletries)	*$*	*$*
Side Hustle Costs (if applicable)	*$*	*$*
Gifts / Donations	*$*	*$*
Total Variable	$	$

Financial Goals this Month

Category	*Amount*
Emergency Fund Savings	*$*
Extra Student Loan Payment	*$*
Retirement (e.g., 401k or Roth IRA)	*$*
Fun Money Set Aside	*$*
Total Goals	*$*

Monthly Summary

Total Income: $ ____________________

Total Spent (Fixed + Variable): $ ______________

Amount Left Over: $ ___________

(Income – Total Spent = What you can save, invest, or roll into next month)

Reflection: Did you spend more than planned on dining out? That's okay! Awareness is the first step. Next month, maybe you pack lunch twice a week and redirect that $40 toward your loan. Small shifts create big results.

My Money Goal for This Month:

"This month, I will ____
because I'm building a future where I'm free from debt and full of possibility."

Your name: ____

Month: ____

Remember: ____

You're not just budgeting—**you're designing your life**. Every conscious choice today gives you more freedom tomorrow. Keep going—you've got this!

Month ______________________________

Monthly Take-Home Pay (After Taxes)

$ ____________________

(This is your net income—the amount that actually hits your bank account.)

Fixed Expenses *(Same amount every month)*

Category	*Budgetd Amount*	*Actual Spent*
Rent	$	$
Utilities (electric, water, internet)	$	$
Phone Bill	$	$
Student Loan Payment	$	$
Transportation (car payment, gas, transit pass)	$	$
Insurance (health, car, renters)	$	$
Subscriptions (Spotify, Netflix, etc.)	$	$
Total Fixed	$	$

Variable Expenses (*Changes each month.*)

Category	*Budgeted Amount*	*Actual Spent*
Groceries	$	$
Dining Out / Coffee	$	$
Entertainment (movies, concerts, etc.)	$	$
Shopping (clothes, gadgets, etc.)	$	$
Personal Care (haircut, toiletries)	$	$
Side Hustle Costs (if applicable)	$	$
Gifts / Donations	$	$
Total Variable	$	$

Financial Goals this Month

Category	*Amount*
Emergency Fund Savings	*$*
Extra Student Loan Payment	*$*
Retirement (e.g., 401k or Roth IRA)	*$*
Fun Money Set Aside	*$*
Total Goals	*$*

Monthly Summary

Total Income: $ ____________________

Total Spent (Fixed + Variable): $ ______________

Amount Left Over: $ ___________

(Income – Total Spent = What you can save, invest, or roll into next month)

Reflection: Did you spend more than planned on dining out? That's okay! Awareness is the first step. Next month, maybe you pack lunch twice a week and redirect that $40 toward your loan. Small shifts create big results.

My Money Goal for This Month:

"This month, I will____
because I'm building a future where I'm free from debt and full of possibility."

Your name: ____

Month: ____

Remember: ____

You're not just budgeting—**you're designing your life**. Every conscious choice today gives you more freedom tomorrow. Keep going—you've got this!

Month ______________________________

Monthly Take-Home Pay (After Taxes)

$ ______________________

(This is your net income—the amount that actually hits your bank account.)

Fixed Expenses *(Same amount every month)*

Category	*Budgetd Amount*	*Actual Spent*
Rent	$	$
Utilities (electric, water, internet)	$	$
Phone Bill	$	$
Student Loan Payment	$	$
Transportation (car payment, gas, transit pass)	$	$
Insurance (health, car, renters)	$	$
Subscriptions (Spotify, Netflix, etc.)	$	$
Total Fixed	$	$

Variable Expenses (*Changes each month.*)

Category	*Budgeted Amount*	*Actual Spent*
Groceries	$	$
Dining Out / Coffee	$	$
Entertainment (movies, concerts, etc.)	$	$
Shopping (clothes, gadgets, etc.)	$	$
Personal Care (haircut, toiletries)	$	$
Side Hustle Costs (if applicable)	$	$
Gifts / Donations	$	$
Total Variable	$	$

Financial Goals this Month

Category	*Amount*
Emergency Fund Savings	*$*
Extra Student Loan Payment	*$*
Retirement (e.g., 401k or Roth IRA)	*$*
Fun Money Set Aside	*$*
Total Goals	*$*

Monthly Summary

Total Income: $ ____________________

Total Spent (Fixed + Variable): $ ______________

Amount Left Over: $ ___________

(Income – Total Spent = What you can save, invest, or roll into next month)

Reflection: Did you spend more than planned on dining out? That's okay! Awareness is the first step. Next month, maybe you pack lunch twice a week and redirect that $40 toward your loan. Small shifts create big results.

My Money Goal for This Month:

"This month, I will ____
because I'm building a future where I'm free from debt and full of possibility."

Your name: ____

Month: ____

Remember: ____

You're not just budgeting—**you're designing your life**. Every conscious choice today gives you more freedom tomorrow. Keep going—you've got this!

Month ________________________________

Monthly Take-Home Pay (After Taxes)

$ ______________________

(This is your net income—the amount that actually hits your bank account.)

Fixed Expenses *(Same amount every month)*

Category	*Budgetd Amount*	*Actual Spent*
Rent	*$*	*$*
Utilities (electric, water, internet)	*$*	*$*
Phone Bill	*$*	*$*
Student Loan Payment	*$*	*$*
Transportation (car payment, gas, transit pass)	*$*	*$*
Insurance (health, car, renters)	*$*	*$*
Subscriptions (Spotify, Netflix, etc.)	*$*	*$*
Total Fixed	*$*	*$*

Variable Expenses (*Changes each month.*)

Category	*Budgeted Amount*	*Actual Spent*
Groceries	*$*	*$*
Dining Out / Coffee	*$*	*$*
Entertainment (movies, concerts, etc.)	*$*	*$*
Shopping (clothes, gadgets, etc.)	*$*	*$*
Personal Care (haircut, toiletries)	*$*	*$*
Side Hustle Costs (if applicable)	*$*	*$*
Gifts / Donations	*$*	*$*
Total Variable	$	$

Financial Goals this Month

Category	*Amount*
Emergency Fund Savings	*$*
Extra Student Loan Payment	*$*
Retirement (e.g., 401k or Roth IRA)	*$*
Fun Money Set Aside	*$*
Total Goals	*$*

Monthly Summary

Total Income: $ ________________________

Total Spent (Fixed + Variable): $ ________________

Amount Left Over: $ ______________

(Income – Total Spent = What you can save, invest, or roll into next month)

Reflection: Did you spend more than planned on dining out? That's okay! Awareness is the first step. Next month, maybe you pack lunch twice a week and redirect that $40 toward your loan. Small shifts create big results.

My Money Goal for This Month:

"This month, I will____ because I'm building a future where I'm free from debt and full of possibility."

Your name: ____

Month: ____

Remember: ____

You're not just budgeting—**you're designing your life**. Every conscious choice today gives you more freedom tomorrow. Keep going—you've got this!

Month ____________________

Monthly Take-Home Pay (After Taxes)

$ ____________________

(This is your net income—the amount that actually hits your bank account.)

Fixed Expenses *(Same amount every month)*

Category	*Budgetd Amount*	*Actual Spent*
Rent	*$*	*$*
Utilities (electric, water, internet)	*$*	*$*
Phone Bill	*$*	*$*
Student Loan Payment	*$*	*$*
Transportation (car payment, gas, transit pass)	*$*	*$*
Insurance (health, car, renters)	*$*	*$*
Subscriptions (Spotify, Netflix, etc.)	*$*	*$*
Total Fixed	*$*	*$*

Variable Expenses (*Changes each month.*)

Category	*Budgeted Amount*	*Actual Spent*
Groceries	*$*	*$*
Dining Out / Coffee	*$*	*$*
Entertainment (movies, concerts, etc.)	*$*	*$*
Shopping (clothes, gadgets, etc.)	*$*	*$*
Personal Care (haircut, toiletries)	*$*	*$*
Side Hustle Costs (if applicable)	*$*	*$*
Gifts / Donations	*$*	*$*
Total Variable	$	$

Financial Goals this Month

Category	*Amount*
Emergency Fund Savings	*$*
Extra Student Loan Payment	*$*
Retirement (e.g., 401k or Roth IRA)	*$*
Fun Money Set Aside	*$*
Total Goals	*$*

Monthly Summary

Total Income: $ ____________________

Total Spent (Fixed + Variable): $ ______________

Amount Left Over: $ ___________

(Income – Total Spent = What you can save, invest, or roll into next month)

Reflection: Did you spend more than planned on dining out? That's okay! Awareness is the first step. Next month, maybe you pack lunch twice a week and redirect that $40 toward your loan. Small shifts create big results.

My Money Goal for This Month:

"This month, I will ____
because I'm building a future where I'm free from debt and full of possibility."

Your name: ____

Month: ____

Remember: ____

You're not just budgeting—**you're designing your life**. Every conscious choice today gives you more freedom tomorrow. Keep going—you've got this!

Month ______________________________

Monthly Take-Home Pay (After Taxes)

$ ____________________

(This is your net income—the amount that actually hits your bank account.)

Fixed Expenses *(Same amount every month)*

Category	*Budgetd Amount*	*Actual Spent*
Rent	*$*	*$*
Utilities (electric, water, internet)	*$*	*$*
Phone Bill	*$*	*$*
Student Loan Payment	*$*	*$*
Transportation (car payment, gas, transit pass)	*$*	*$*
Insurance (health, car, renters)	*$*	*$*
Subscriptions (Spotify, Netflix, etc.)	*$*	*$*
Total Fixed	*$*	*$*

Variable Expenses (*Changes each month.*)

Category	*Budgeted Amount*	*Actual Spent*
Groceries	*$*	*$*
Dining Out / Coffee	*$*	*$*
Entertainment (movies, concerts, etc.)	*$*	*$*
Shopping (clothes, gadgets, etc.)	*$*	*$*
Personal Care (haircut, toiletries)	*$*	*$*
Side Hustle Costs (if applicable)	*$*	*$*
Gifts / Donations	*$*	*$*
Total Variable	$	$

Financial Goals this Month

Category	*Amount*
Emergency Fund Savings	*$*
Extra Student Loan Payment	*$*
Retirement (e.g., 401k or Roth IRA)	*$*
Fun Money Set Aside	*$*
Total Goals	*$*

Monthly Summary

Total Income: $ ______________________

Total Spent (Fixed + Variable): $ ________________

Amount Left Over: $ _____________

(Income – Total Spent = What you can save, invest, or roll into next month)

Reflection: Did you spend more than planned on dining out? That's okay! Awareness is the first step. Next month, maybe you pack lunch twice a week and redirect that $40 toward your loan. Small shifts create big results.

My Money Goal for This Month:

"This month, I will ____
because I'm building a future where I'm free from debt and full of possibility."

Your name: ____

Month: ____

Remember: ____

You're not just budgeting—**you're designing your life**. Every conscious choice today gives you more freedom tomorrow. Keep going—you've got this!

Month ______________________________

Monthly Take-Home Pay (After Taxes)

$ ____________________

(This is your net income—the amount that actually hits your bank account.)

Fixed Expenses *(Same amount every month)*

Category	*Budgetd Amount*	*Actual Spent*
Rent	$	$
Utilities (electric, water, internet)	$	$
Phone Bill	$	$
Student Loan Payment	$	$
Transportation (car payment, gas, transit pass)	$	$
Insurance (health, car, renters)	$	$
Subscriptions (Spotify, Netflix, etc.)	$	$
Total Fixed	$	$

Variable Expenses (*Changes each month.*)

Category	*Budgeted Amount*	*Actual Spent*
Groceries	$	$
Dining Out / Coffee	$	$
Entertainment (movies, concerts, etc.)	$	$
Shopping (clothes, gadgets, etc.)	$	$
Personal Care (haircut, toiletries)	$	$
Side Hustle Costs (if applicable)	$	$
Gifts / Donations	$	$
Total Variable	$	$

Financial Goals this Month

Category	*Amount*
Emergency Fund Savings	*$*
Extra Student Loan Payment	*$*
Retirement (e.g., 401k or Roth IRA)	*$*
Fun Money Set Aside	*$*
Total Goals	*$*

Monthly Summary

Total Income: $ ____________________

Total Spent (Fixed + Variable): $ ______________

Amount Left Over: $ ___________

(Income – Total Spent = What you can save, invest, or roll into next month)

Reflection: Did you spend more than planned on dining out? That's okay! Awareness is the first step. Next month, maybe you pack lunch twice a week and redirect that $40 toward your loan. Small shifts create big results.

My Money Goal for This Month:

"This month, I will ____
because I'm building a future where I'm free from debt and full of possibility."

Your name: ____

Month: ____

Remember: ____

You're not just budgeting—**you're designing your life**. Every conscious choice today gives you more freedom tomorrow. Keep going—you've got this!

Month ____________________

Monthly Take-Home Pay (After Taxes)

$ ____________________

(This is your net income—the amount that actually hits your bank account.)

Fixed Expenses *(Same amount every month)*

Category	*Budgetd Amount*	*Actual Spent*
Rent	$	$
Utilities (electric, water, internet)	$	$
Phone Bill	$	$
Student Loan Payment	$	$
Transportation (car payment, gas, transit pass)	$	$
Insurance (health, car, renters)	$	$
Subscriptions (Spotify, Netflix, etc.)	$	$
Total Fixed	$	$

Variable Expenses (*Changes each month.*)

Category	*Budgeted Amount*	*Actual Spent*
Groceries	$	$
Dining Out / Coffee	$	$
Entertainment (movies, concerts, etc.)	$	$
Shopping (clothes, gadgets, etc.)	$	$
Personal Care (haircut, toiletries)	$	$
Side Hustle Costs (if applicable)	$	$
Gifts / Donations	$	$
Total Variable	$	$

Financial Goals this Month

Category	*Amount*
Emergency Fund Savings	*$*
Extra Student Loan Payment	*$*
Retirement (e.g., 401k or Roth IRA)	*$*
Fun Money Set Aside	*$*
Total Goals	*$*

Monthly Summary

Total Income: $ ______________________

Total Spent (Fixed + Variable): $ ________________

Amount Left Over: $ _____________

(Income – Total Spent = What you can save, invest, or roll into next month)

Reflection: Did you spend more than planned on dining out? That's okay! Awareness is the first step. Next month, maybe you pack lunch twice a week and redirect that $40 toward your loan. Small shifts create big results.

My Money Goal for This Month:

"This month, I will ____
because I'm building a future where I'm free from debt and full of possibility."

Your name: ____

Month: ____

Remember: ____

You're not just budgeting—**you're designing your life**. Every conscious choice today gives you more freedom tomorrow. Keep going—you've got this!

Month ______________________________

Monthly Take-Home Pay (After Taxes)

$ ______________________

(This is your net income—the amount that actually hits your bank account.)

Fixed Expenses *(Same amount every month)*

Category	*Budgetd Amount*	*Actual Spent*
Rent	*$*	*$*
Utilities (electric, water, internet)	*$*	*$*
Phone Bill	*$*	*$*
Student Loan Payment	*$*	*$*
Transportation (car payment, gas, transit pass)	*$*	*$*
Insurance (health, car, renters)	*$*	*$*
Subscriptions (Spotify, Netflix, etc.)	*$*	*$*
Total Fixed	*$*	*$*

Variable Expenses (*Changes each month.*)

Category	*Budgeted Amount*	*Actual Spent*
Groceries	*$*	*$*
Dining Out / Coffee	*$*	*$*
Entertainment (movies, concerts, etc.)	*$*	*$*
Shopping (clothes, gadgets, etc.)	*$*	*$*
Personal Care (haircut, toiletries)	*$*	*$*
Side Hustle Costs (if applicable)	*$*	*$*
Gifts / Donations	*$*	*$*
Total Variable	$	$

Financial Goals this Month

Category	*Amount*
Emergency Fund Savings	*$*
Extra Student Loan Payment	*$*
Retirement (e.g., 401k or Roth IRA)	*$*
Fun Money Set Aside	*$*
Total Goals	*$*

Monthly Summary

Total Income: $ ____________________

Total Spent (Fixed + Variable): $ ______________

Amount Left Over: $ ___________

(Income – Total Spent = What you can save, invest, or roll into next month)

Reflection: Did you spend more than planned on dining out? That's okay! Awareness is the first step. Next month, maybe you pack lunch twice a week and redirect that $40 toward your loan. Small shifts create big results.

My Money Goal for This Month:

"This month, I will____
because I'm building a future where I'm free from debt and full of possibility."

Your name: ____

Month: ____

Remember: ____

You're not just budgeting—**you're designing your life**. Every conscious choice today gives you more freedom tomorrow. Keep going—you've got this!

Month ________________________________

Monthly Take-Home Pay (After Taxes)

$ ______________________

(This is your net income—the amount that actually hits your bank account.)

Fixed Expenses *(Same amount every month)*

Category	*Budgetd Amount*	*Actual Spent*
Rent	$	$
Utilities (electric, water, internet)	$	$
Phone Bill	$	$
Student Loan Payment	$	$
Transportation (car payment, gas, transit pass)	$	$
Insurance (health, car, renters)	$	$
Subscriptions (Spotify, Netflix, etc.)	$	$
Total Fixed	$	$

Variable Expenses (*Changes each month.*)

Category	*Budgeted Amount*	*Actual Spent*
Groceries	$	$
Dining Out / Coffee	$	$
Entertainment (movies, concerts, etc.)	$	$
Shopping (clothes, gadgets, etc.)	$	$
Personal Care (haircut, toiletries)	$	$
Side Hustle Costs (if applicable)	$	$
Gifts / Donations	$	$
Total Variable	$	$

Financial Goals this Month

Category	*Amount*
Emergency Fund Savings	*$*
Extra Student Loan Payment	*$*
Retirement (e.g., 401k or Roth IRA)	*$*
Fun Money Set Aside	*$*
Total Goals	*$*

Monthly Summary

Total Income: $ ______________________________

Total Spent (Fixed + Variable): $ ______________________

Amount Left Over: $ _________________

(Income – Total Spent = What you can save, invest, or roll into next month)

Reflection: Did you spend more than planned on dining out? That's okay! Awareness is the first step. Next month, maybe you pack lunch twice a week and redirect that $40 toward your loan. Small shifts create big results.

My Money Goal for This Month:

"This month, I will ____
because I'm building a future where I'm free from debt and full of possibility."

Your name: ____

Month: ____

Remember: ____

You're not just budgeting—**you're designing your life**. Every conscious choice today gives you more freedom tomorrow. Keep going—you've got this!

Month ______________________________

Monthly Take-Home Pay (After Taxes)

$ ____________________

(This is your net income—the amount that actually hits your bank account.)

Fixed Expenses *(Same amount every month)*

Category	*Budgetd Amount*	*Actual Spent*
Rent	$	$
Utilities (electric, water, internet)	$	$
Phone Bill	$	$
Student Loan Payment	$	$
Transportation (car payment, gas, transit pass)	$	$
Insurance (health, car, renters)	$	$
Subscriptions (Spotify, Netflix, etc.)	$	$
Total Fixed	$	$

Variable Expenses (*Changes each month.*)

Category	*Budgeted Amount*	*Actual Spent*
Groceries	$	$
Dining Out / Coffee	$	$
Entertainment (movies, concerts, etc.)	$	$
Shopping (clothes, gadgets, etc.)	$	$
Personal Care (haircut, toiletries)	$	$
Side Hustle Costs (if applicable)	$	$
Gifts / Donations	$	$
Total Variable	$	$

Financial Goals this Month

Category	*Amount*
Emergency Fund Savings	*$*
Extra Student Loan Payment	*$*
Retirement (e.g., 401k or Roth IRA)	*$*
Fun Money Set Aside	*$*
Total Goals	*$*

Monthly Summary

Total Income: $ ______________________

Total Spent (Fixed + Variable): $ ________________

Amount Left Over: $ ____________

(Income – Total Spent = What you can save, invest, or roll into next month)

Reflection: Did you spend more than planned on dining out? That's okay! Awareness is the first step. Next month, maybe you pack lunch twice a week and redirect that $40 toward your loan. Small shifts create big results.

My Money Goal for This Month:

"This month, I will ____
because I'm building a future where I'm free from debt and full of possibility."

Your name: ____

Month: ____

Remember: ____

You're not just budgeting—**you're designing your life**. Every conscious choice today gives you more freedom tomorrow. Keep going—you've got this!

Month ______________________________

Monthly Take-Home Pay (After Taxes)

$ ____________________

(This is your net income—the amount that actually hits your bank account.)

Fixed Expenses *(Same amount every month)*

Category	*Budgetd Amount*	*Actual Spent*
Rent	*$*	*$*
Utilities (electric, water, internet)	*$*	*$*
Phone Bill	*$*	*$*
Student Loan Payment	*$*	*$*
Transportation (car payment, gas, transit pass)	*$*	*$*
Insurance (health, car, renters)	*$*	*$*
Subscriptions (Spotify, Netflix, etc.)	*$*	*$*
Total Fixed	*$*	*$*

Variable Expenses (*Changes each month.*)

Category	*Budgeted Amount*	*Actual Spent*
Groceries	*$*	*$*
Dining Out / Coffee	*$*	*$*
Entertainment (movies, concerts, etc.)	*$*	*$*
Shopping (clothes, gadgets, etc.)	*$*	*$*
Personal Care (haircut, toiletries)	*$*	*$*
Side Hustle Costs (if applicable)	*$*	*$*
Gifts / Donations	*$*	*$*
Total Variable	$	$

Financial Goals this Month

Category	*Amount*
Emergency Fund Savings	*$*
Extra Student Loan Payment	*$*
Retirement (e.g., 401k or Roth IRA)	*$*
Fun Money Set Aside	*$*
Total Goals	*$*

Monthly Summary

Total Income: $ ____________________

Total Spent (Fixed + Variable): $ ______________

Amount Left Over: $ ___________

(Income – Total Spent = What you can save, invest, or roll into next month)

Reflection: Did you spend more than planned on dining out? That's okay! Awareness is the first step. Next month, maybe you pack lunch twice a week and redirect that $40 toward your loan. Small shifts create big results.

My Money Goal for This Month:

"This month, I will____
because I'm building a future where I'm free from debt and full of possibility."

Your name: ____

Month: ____

Remember: ____

You're not just budgeting—**you're designing your life**. Every conscious choice today gives you more freedom tomorrow. Keep going—you've got this!

Month ____

Monthly Take-Home Pay (After Taxes)

$ ______________________

(This is your net income—the amount that actually hits your bank account.)

Fixed Expenses *(Same amount every month)*

Category	*Budgetd Amount*	*Actual Spent*
Rent	*$*	*$*
Utilities (electric, water, internet)	*$*	*$*
Phone Bill	*$*	*$*
Student Loan Payment	*$*	*$*
Transportation (car payment, gas, transit pass)	*$*	*$*
Insurance (health, car, renters)	*$*	*$*
Subscriptions (Spotify, Netflix, etc.)	*$*	*$*
Total Fixed	*$*	*$*

Variable Expenses (*Changes each month.*)

Category	*Budgeted Amount*	*Actual Spent*
Groceries	*$*	*$*
Dining Out / Coffee	*$*	*$*
Entertainment (movies, concerts, etc.)	*$*	*$*
Shopping (clothes, gadgets, etc.)	*$*	*$*
Personal Care (haircut, toiletries)	*$*	*$*
Side Hustle Costs (if applicable)	*$*	*$*
Gifts / Donations	*$*	*$*
Total Variable	$	$

Financial Goals this Month

Category	*Amount*
Emergency Fund Savings	*$*
Extra Student Loan Payment	*$*
Retirement (e.g., 401k or Roth IRA)	*$*
Fun Money Set Aside	*$*
Total Goals	*$*

Monthly Summary

Total Income: $ ______________________

Total Spent (Fixed + Variable): $ ________________

Amount Left Over: $ _____________

(Income – Total Spent = What you can save, invest, or roll into next month)

Reflection: Did you spend more than planned on dining out? That's okay! Awareness is the first step. Next month, maybe you pack lunch twice a week and redirect that $40 toward your loan. Small shifts create big results.

My Money Goal for This Month:

"This month, I will ____
because I'm building a future where I'm free from debt and full of possibility."

Your name: ____

Month: ____

Remember: ____

You're not just budgeting—**you're designing your life**. Every conscious choice today gives you more freedom tomorrow. Keep going—you've got this!

Month ______________________________

Monthly Take-Home Pay (After Taxes)

$ ____________________

(This is your net income—the amount that actually hits your bank account.)

Fixed Expenses *(Same amount every month)*

Category	*Budgetd Amount*	*Actual Spent*
Rent	*$*	*$*
Utilities (electric, water, internet)	*$*	*$*
Phone Bill	*$*	*$*
Student Loan Payment	*$*	*$*
Transportation (car payment, gas, transit pass)	*$*	*$*
Insurance (health, car, renters)	*$*	*$*
Subscriptions (Spotify, Netflix, etc.)	*$*	*$*
Total Fixed	*$*	*$*

Variable Expenses (*Changes each month.*)

Category	*Budgeted Amount*	*Actual Spent*
Groceries	*$*	*$*
Dining Out / Coffee	*$*	*$*
Entertainment (movies, concerts, etc.)	*$*	*$*
Shopping (clothes, gadgets, etc.)	*$*	*$*
Personal Care (haircut, toiletries)	*$*	*$*
Side Hustle Costs (if applicable)	*$*	*$*
Gifts / Donations	*$*	*$*
Total Variable	$	$

Financial Goals this Month

Category	*Amount*
Emergency Fund Savings	*$*
Extra Student Loan Payment	*$*
Retirement (e.g., 401k or Roth IRA)	*$*
Fun Money Set Aside	*$*
Total Goals	*$*

Monthly Summary

Total Income: $ ____________________

Total Spent (Fixed + Variable): $ ____________________

Amount Left Over: $ ________________

(Income – Total Spent = What you can save, invest, or roll into next month)

Reflection: Did you spend more than planned on dining out? That's okay! Awareness is the first step. Next month, maybe you pack lunch twice a week and redirect that $40 toward your loan. Small shifts create big results.

My Money Goal for This Month:

"This month, I will ____
because I'm building a future where I'm free from debt and full of possibility."

Your name: ____

Month: ____

Remember: ____

You're not just budgeting—**you're designing your life**. Every conscious choice today gives you more freedom tomorrow. Keep going—you've got this!

Month ______________________________

Monthly Take-Home Pay (After Taxes)

$ ____________________

(This is your net income—the amount that actually hits your bank account.)

Fixed Expenses *(Same amount every month)*

Category	*Budgetd Amount*	*Actual Spent*
Rent	*$*	*$*
Utilities (electric, water, internet)	*$*	*$*
Phone Bill	*$*	*$*
Student Loan Payment	*$*	*$*
Transportation (car payment, gas, transit pass)	*$*	*$*
Insurance (health, car, renters)	*$*	*$*
Subscriptions (Spotify, Netflix, etc.)	*$*	*$*
Total Fixed	*$*	*$*

Variable Expenses (*Changes each month.*)

Category	*Budgeted Amount*	*Actual Spent*
Groceries	*$*	*$*
Dining Out / Coffee	*$*	*$*
Entertainment (movies, concerts, etc.)	*$*	*$*
Shopping (clothes, gadgets, etc.)	*$*	*$*
Personal Care (haircut, toiletries)	*$*	*$*
Side Hustle Costs (if applicable)	*$*	*$*
Gifts / Donations	*$*	*$*
Total Variable	**$**	**$**

Financial Goals this Month

Category	*Amount*
Emergency Fund Savings	*$*
Extra Student Loan Payment	*$*
Retirement (e.g., 401k or Roth IRA)	*$*
Fun Money Set Aside	*$*
Total Goals	*$*

Monthly Summary

Total Income: $ ____________________

Total Spent (Fixed + Variable): $ ______________

Amount Left Over: $ ____________

(Income – Total Spent = What you can save, invest, or roll into next month)

Reflection: Did you spend more than planned on dining out? That's okay! Awareness is the first step. Next month, maybe you pack lunch twice a week and redirect that $40 toward your loan. Small shifts create big results.

My Money Goal for This Month:

"This month, I will ____
because I'm building a future where I'm free from debt and full of possibility."

Your name: ____

Month: ____

Remember: ____

You're not just budgeting—**you're designing your life**. Every conscious choice today gives you more freedom tomorrow. Keep going—you've got this!

Month ______________________________

Monthly Take-Home Pay (After Taxes)

$ ____________________

(This is your net income—the amount that actually hits your bank account.)

Fixed Expenses *(Same amount every month)*

Category	*Budgetd Amount*	*Actual Spent*
Rent	*$*	*$*
Utilities (electric, water, internet)	*$*	*$*
Phone Bill	*$*	*$*
Student Loan Payment	*$*	*$*
Transportation (car payment, gas, transit pass)	*$*	*$*
Insurance (health, car, renters)	*$*	*$*
Subscriptions (Spotify, Netflix, etc.)	*$*	*$*
Total Fixed	*$*	*$*

Variable Expenses (*Changes each month.*)

Category	*Budgeted Amount*	*Actual Spent*
Groceries	*$*	*$*
Dining Out / Coffee	*$*	*$*
Entertainment (movies, concerts, etc.)	*$*	*$*
Shopping (clothes, gadgets, etc.)	*$*	*$*
Personal Care (haircut, toiletries)	*$*	*$*
Side Hustle Costs (if applicable)	*$*	*$*
Gifts / Donations	*$*	*$*
Total Variable	$	$

Financial Goals this Month

Category	*Amount*
Emergency Fund Savings	*$*
Extra Student Loan Payment	*$*
Retirement (e.g., 401k or Roth IRA)	*$*
Fun Money Set Aside	*$*
Total Goals	*$*

Monthly Summary

Total Income: $ ____________________

Total Spent (Fixed + Variable): $ ______________

Amount Left Over: $ ____________

(Income – Total Spent = What you can save, invest, or roll into next month)

Reflection: Did you spend more than planned on dining out? That's okay! Awareness is the first step. Next month, maybe you pack lunch twice a week and redirect that $40 toward your loan. Small shifts create big results.

My Money Good for This Month:

"This month, I will ____
because I'm building a future where I'm free from debt and full of possibility."

Your name: ____

Month: ____

Remember: ____

You're not just budgeting—**you're designing your life**. Every conscious choice today gives you more freedom tomorrow. Keep going—you've got this!

Month ______________________________

Monthly Take-Home Pay (After Taxes)

$ ____________________

(This is your net income—the amount that actually hits your bank account.)

Fixed Expenses *(Same amount every month)*

Category	*Budgetd Amount*	*Actual Spent*
Rent	$	$
Utilities (electric, water, internet)	$	$
Phone Bill	$	$
Student Loan Payment	$	$
Transportation (car payment, gas, transit pass)	$	$
Insurance (health, car, renters)	$	$
Subscriptions (Spotify, Netflix, etc.)	$	$
Total Fixed	$	$

Variable Expenses (*Changes each month.*)

Category	*Budgeted Amount*	*Actual Spent*
Groceries	$	$
Dining Out / Coffee	$	$
Entertainment (movies, concerts, etc.)	$	$
Shopping (clothes, gadgets, etc.)	$	$
Personal Care (haircut, toiletries)	$	$
Side Hustle Costs (if applicable)	$	$
Gifts / Donations	$	$
Total Variable	$	$

Financial Goals this Month

Category	*Amount*
Emergency Fund Savings	*$*
Extra Student Loan Payment	*$*
Retirement (e.g., 401k or Roth IRA)	*$*
Fun Money Set Aside	*$*
Total Goals	*$*

Monthly Summary

Total Income: $ ______________________

Total Spent (Fixed + Variable): $ ________________

Amount Left Over: $ _____________

(Income – Total Spent = What you can save, invest, or roll into next month)

Reflection: Did you spend more than planned on dining out? That's okay! Awareness is the first step. Next month, maybe you pack lunch twice a week and redirect that $40 toward your loan. Small shifts create big results.

My Money Goal for This Month:

"This month, I will ____
because I'm building a future where I'm free from debt and full of possibility."

Your name: ____

Month: ____

Remember: ____

You're not just budgeting—**you're designing your life**. Every conscious choice today gives you more freedom tomorrow. Keep going—you've got this!

Month ________________________________

Monthly Take-Home Pay (After Taxes)

$ ____________________

(This is your net income—the amount that actually hits your bank account.)

Fixed Expenses *(Same amount every month)*

Category	*Budgetd Amount*	*Actual Spent*
Rent	*$*	*$*
Utilities (electric, water, internet)	*$*	*$*
Phone Bill	*$*	*$*
Student Loan Payment	*$*	*$*
Transportation (car payment, gas, transit pass)	*$*	*$*
Insurance (health, car, renters)	*$*	*$*
Subscriptions (Spotify, Netflix, etc.)	*$*	*$*
Total Fixed	*$*	*$*

Variable Expenses (*Changes each month.*)

Category	*Budgeted Amount*	*Actual Spent*
Groceries	*$*	*$*
Dining Out / Coffee	*$*	*$*
Entertainment (movies, concerts, etc.)	*$*	*$*
Shopping (clothes, gadgets, etc.)	*$*	*$*
Personal Care (haircut, toiletries)	*$*	*$*
Side Hustle Costs (if applicable)	*$*	*$*
Gifts / Donations	*$*	*$*
Total Variable	$	$

Financial Goals this Month

Category	Amount
Emergency Fund Savings	*$*
Extra Student Loan Payment	*$*
Retirement (e.g., 401k or Roth IRA)	*$*
Fun Money Set Aside	*$*
Total Goals	*$*

Monthly Summary

Total Income: $ ______________________

Total Spent (Fixed + Variable): $ ________________

Amount Left Over: $ _____________

(Income – Total Spent = What you can save, invest, or roll into next month)

Reflection: Did you spend more than planned on dining out? That's okay! Awareness is the first step. Next month, maybe you pack lunch twice a week and redirect that $40 toward your loan. Small shifts create big results.

My Money Goal for This Month:

*"This month, I will*____
because I'm building a future where I'm free from debt and full of possibility."

Your name: ____

Month: ____

Remember: ____

You're not just budgeting—**you're designing your life**. Every conscious choice today gives you more freedom tomorrow. Keep going—you've got this!

Month ______________________________

Monthly Take-Home Pay (After Taxes)

$ ____________________

(This is your net income—the amount that actually hits your bank account.)

Fixed Expenses *(Same amount every month)*

Category	*Budgetd Amount*	*Actual Spent*
Rent	$	$
Utilities (electric, water, internet)	$	$
Phone Bill	$	$
Student Loan Payment	$	$
Transportation (car payment, gas, transit pass)	$	$
Insurance (health, car, renters)	$	$
Subscriptions (Spotify, Netflix, etc.)	$	$
Total Fixed	$	$

Variable Expenses (*Changes each month.*)

Category	*Budgeted Amount*	*Actual Spent*
Groceries	$	$
Dining Out / Coffee	$	$
Entertainment (movies, concerts, etc.)	$	$
Shopping (clothes, gadgets, etc.)	$	$
Personal Care (haircut, toiletries)	$	$
Side Hustle Costs (if applicable)	$	$
Gifts / Donations	$	$
Total Variable	$	$

Financial Goals this Month

Category	*Amount*
Emergency Fund Savings	*$*
Extra Student Loan Payment	*$*
Retirement (e.g., 401k or Roth IRA)	*$*
Fun Money Set Aside	*$*
Total Goals	*$*

Monthly Summary

Total Income: $ ____________________

Total Spent (Fixed + Variable): $ ______________

Amount Left Over: $ ____________

(Income – Total Spent = What you can save, invest, or roll into next month)

Reflection: Did you spend more than planned on dining out? That's okay! Awareness is the first step. Next month, maybe you pack lunch twice a week and redirect that $40 toward your loan. Small shifts create big results.

My Money Goal for This Month:

"This month, I will ____
because I'm building a future where I'm free from debt and full of possibility."

Your name: ____

Month: ____

Remember: ____

You're not just budgeting—**you're designing your life**. Every conscious choice today gives you more freedom tomorrow. Keep going—you've got this!

Month ____

Monthly Take-Home Pay (After Taxes)

$ _________________________

(This is your net income—the amount that actually hits your bank account.)

Fixed Expenses *(Same amount every month)*

Category	*Budgetd Amount*	*Actual Spent*
Rent	*$*	*$*
Utilities (electric, water, internet)	*$*	*$*
Phone Bill	*$*	*$*
Student Loan Payment	*$*	*$*
Transportation (car payment, gas, transit pass)	*$*	*$*
Insurance (health, car, renters)	*$*	*$*
Subscriptions (Spotify, Netflix, etc.)	*$*	*$*
Total Fixed	*$*	*$*

Variable Expenses (*Changes each month.*)

Category	*Budgeted Amount*	*Actual Spent*
Groceries	*$*	*$*
Dining Out / Coffee	*$*	*$*
Entertainment (movies, concerts, etc.)	*$*	*$*
Shopping (clothes, gadgets, etc.)	*$*	*$*
Personal Care (haircut, toiletries)	*$*	*$*
Side Hustle Costs (if applicable)	*$*	*$*
Gifts / Donations	*$*	*$*
Total Variable	$	$

Financial Goals this Month

Category	*Amount*
Emergency Fund Savings	$
Extra Student Loan Payment	$
Retirement (e.g., 401k or Roth IRA)	$
Fun Money Set Aside	$
Total Goals	$

Monthly Summary

Total Income: $ ______________________

Total Spent (Fixed + Variable): $ ________________

Amount Left Over: $ _____________

(Income – Total Spent = What you can save, invest, or roll into next month)

Reflection: Did you spend more than planned on dining out? That's okay! Awareness is the first step. Next month, maybe you pack lunch twice a week and redirect that $40 toward your loan. Small shifts create big results.

My Money Goal for This Month:

"This month, I will ____
because I'm building a future where I'm free from debt and full of possibility."

Your name: ____

Month: ____

Remember: ____

You're not just budgeting—**you're designing your life**. Every conscious choice today gives you more freedom tomorrow. Keep going—you've got this!

Month ____________________________________

Monthly Take-Home Pay (After Taxes)

$ ____________________

(This is your net income—the amount that actually hits your bank account.)

Fixed Expenses *(Same amount every month)*

Category	*Budgetd Amount*	*Actual Spent*
Rent	$	$
Utilities (electric, water, internet)	$	$
Phone Bill	$	$
Student Loan Payment	$	$
Transportation (car payment, gas, transit pass)	$	$
Insurance (health, car, renters)	$	$
Subscriptions (Spotify, Netflix, etc.)	$	$
Total Fixed	$	$

Variable Expenses (*Changes each month.*)

Category	*Budgeted Amount*	*Actual Spent*
Groceries	$	$
Dining Out / Coffee	$	$
Entertainment (movies, concerts, etc.)	$	$
Shopping (clothes, gadgets, etc.)	$	$
Personal Care (haircut, toiletries)	$	$
Side Hustle Costs (if applicable)	$	$
Gifts / Donations	$	$
Total Variable	$	$

Financial Goals this Month

Category	*Amount*
Emergency Fund Savings	*$*
Extra Student Loan Payment	*$*
Retirement (e.g., 401k or Roth IRA)	*$*
Fun Money Set Aside	*$*
Total Goals	*$*

Monthly Summary

Total Income: $ ____________________

Total Spent (Fixed + Variable): $ ______________

Amount Left Over: $ ___________

(Income – Total Spent = What you can save, invest, or roll into next month)

Reflection: Did you spend more than planned on dining out? That's okay! Awareness is the first step. Next month, maybe you pack lunch twice a week and redirect that $40 toward your loan. Small shifts create big results.

My Money Goal for This Month:

"This month, I will ____
because I'm building a future where I'm free from debt and full of possibility."

Your name: ____

Month: ____

Remember: ____

You're not just budgeting—**you're designing your life**. Every conscious choice today gives you more freedom tomorrow. Keep going—you've got this!

Month ______________________________

Monthly Take-Home Pay (After Taxes)

$ ____________________

(This is your net income—the amount that actually hits your bank account.)

Fixed Expenses *(Same amount every month)*

Category	*Budgetd Amount*	*Actual Spent*
Rent	*$*	*$*
Utilities (electric, water, internet)	*$*	*$*
Phone Bill	*$*	*$*
Student Loan Payment	*$*	*$*
Transportation (car payment, gas, transit pass)	*$*	*$*
Insurance (health, car, renters)	*$*	*$*
Subscriptions (Spotify, Netflix, etc.)	*$*	*$*
Total Fixed	*$*	*$*

Variable Expenses (*Changes each month.*)

Category	*Budgeted Amount*	*Actual Spent*
Groceries	*$*	*$*
Dining Out / Coffee	*$*	*$*
Entertainment (movies, concerts, etc.)	*$*	*$*
Shopping (clothes, gadgets, etc.)	*$*	*$*
Personal Care (haircut, toiletries)	*$*	*$*
Side Hustle Costs (if applicable)	*$*	*$*
Gifts / Donations	*$*	*$*
Total Variable	$	$

Financial Goals this Month

Category	*Amount*
Emergency Fund Savings	*$*
Extra Student Loan Payment	*$*
Retirement (e.g., 401k or Roth IRA)	*$*
Fun Money Set Aside	*$*
Total Goals	*$*

Monthly Summary

Total Income: $ ______________________

Total Spent (Fixed + Variable): $ ________________

Amount Left Over: $ _____________

(Income – Total Spent = What you can save, invest, or roll into next month)

Reflection: Did you spend more than planned on dining out? That's okay! Awareness is the first step. Next month, maybe you pack lunch twice a week and redirect that $40 toward your loan. Small shifts create big results.

My Money Goal for This Month:

"This month, I will ____
because I'm building a future where I'm free from debt and full of possibility."

Your name: ____

Month: ____

Remember: ____

You're not just budgeting—**you're designing your life**. Every conscious choice today gives you more freedom tomorrow. Keep going—you've got this!

Month ________________________________

Monthly Take-Home Pay (After Taxes)

$ ______________________

(This is your net income—the amount that actually hits your bank account.)

Fixed Expenses *(Same amount every month)*

Category	*Budgetd Amount*	*Actual Spent*
Rent	*$*	*$*
Utilities (electric, water, internet)	*$*	*$*
Phone Bill	*$*	*$*
Student Loan Payment	*$*	*$*
Transportation (car payment, gas, transit pass)	*$*	*$*
Insurance (health, car, renters)	*$*	*$*
Subscriptions (Spotify, Netflix, etc.)	*$*	*$*
Total Fixed	*$*	*$*

Variable Expenses (*Changes each month.*)

Category	*Budgeted Amount*	*Actual Spent*
Groceries	*$*	*$*
Dining Out / Coffee	*$*	*$*
Entertainment (movies, concerts, etc.)	*$*	*$*
Shopping (clothes, gadgets, etc.)	*$*	*$*
Personal Care (haircut, toiletries)	*$*	*$*
Side Hustle Costs (if applicable)	*$*	*$*
Gifts / Donations	*$*	*$*
Total Variable	$	$

Financial Goals this Month

Category	*Amount*
Emergency Fund Savings	*$*
Extra Student Loan Payment	*$*
Retirement (e.g., 401k or Roth IRA)	*$*
Fun Money Set Aside	*$*
Total Goals	*$*

Monthly Summary

Total Income: $ ______________________

Total Spent (Fixed + Variable): $ ________________

Amount Left Over: $ _____________

(Income – Total Spent = What you can save, invest, or roll into next month)

Reflection: Did you spend more than planned on dining out? That's okay! Awareness is the first step. Next month, maybe you pack lunch twice a week and redirect that $40 toward your loan. Small shifts create big results.

My Money Goal for This Month:

"This month, I will ____
because I'm building a future where I'm free from debt and full of possibility."

Your name: ____

Month: ____

Remember: ____

You're not just budgeting—**you're designing your life**. Every conscious choice today gives you more freedom tomorrow. Keep going—you've got this!

Month ______________________________________

Monthly Take-Home Pay (After Taxes)

$ _______________________

(This is your net income—the amount that actually hits your bank account.)

Fixed Expenses *(Same amount every month)*

Category	*Budgetd Amount*	*Actual Spent*
Rent	*$*	*$*
Utilities (electric, water, internet)	*$*	*$*
Phone Bill	*$*	*$*
Student Loan Payment	*$*	*$*
Transportation (car payment, gas, transit pass)	*$*	*$*
Insurance (health, car, renters)	*$*	*$*
Subscriptions (Spotify, Netflix, etc.)	*$*	*$*
Total Fixed	*$*	*$*

Variable Expenses (*Changes each month.*)

Category	*Budgeted Amount*	*Actual Spent*
Groceries	*$*	*$*
Dining Out / Coffee	*$*	*$*
Entertainment (movies, concerts, etc.)	*$*	*$*
Shopping (clothes, gadgets, etc.)	*$*	*$*
Personal Care (haircut, toiletries)	*$*	*$*
Side Hustle Costs (if applicable)	*$*	*$*
Gifts / Donations	*$*	*$*
Total Variable	$	$

Financial Goals this Month

Category	*Amount*
Emergency Fund Savings	*$*
Extra Student Loan Payment	*$*
Retirement (e.g., 401k or Roth IRA)	*$*
Fun Money Set Aside	*$*
Total Goals	*$*

Monthly Summary

Total Income: $ ______________________

Total Spent (Fixed + Variable): $ ________________

Amount Left Over: $ _____________

(Income – Total Spent = What you can save, invest, or roll into next month)

Reflection: Did you spend more than planned on dining out? That's okay! Awareness is the first step. Next month, maybe you pack lunch twice a week and redirect that $40 toward your loan. Small shifts create big results.

My Money Goal for This Month:

"This month, I will ____
because I'm building a future where I'm free from debt and full of possibility."

Your name: ____

Month: ____

Remember: ____

You're not just budgeting—**you're designing your life**. Every conscious choice today gives you more freedom tomorrow. Keep going—you've got this!

Month ______________________________

Monthly Take-Home Pay (After Taxes)

$ ____________________

(This is your net income—the amount that actually hits your bank account.)

Fixed Expenses *(Same amount every month)*

Category	*Budgetd Amount*	*Actual Spent*
Rent	*$*	*$*
Utilities (electric, water, internet)	*$*	*$*
Phone Bill	*$*	*$*
Student Loan Payment	*$*	*$*
Transportation (car payment, gas, transit pass)	*$*	*$*
Insurance (health, car, renters)	*$*	*$*
Subscriptions (Spotify, Netflix, etc.)	*$*	*$*
Total Fixed	*$*	*$*

Variable Expenses (*Changes each month.*)

Category	*Budgeted Amount*	*Actual Spent*
Groceries	*$*	*$*
Dining Out / Coffee	*$*	*$*
Entertainment (movies, concerts, etc.)	*$*	*$*
Shopping (clothes, gadgets, etc.)	*$*	*$*
Personal Care (haircut, toiletries)	*$*	*$*
Side Hustle Costs (if applicable)	*$*	*$*
Gifts / Donations	*$*	*$*
Total Variable	$	$

Financial Goals this Month

Category	*Amount*
Emergency Fund Savings	*$*
Extra Student Loan Payment	*$*
Retirement (e.g., 401k or Roth IRA)	*$*
Fun Money Set Aside	*$*
Total Goals	*$*

Monthly Summary

Total Income: $ ____________________

Total Spent (Fixed + Variable): $ ______________

Amount Left Over: $ ___________

(Income – Total Spent = What you can save, invest, or roll into next month)

Reflection: Did you spend more than planned on dining out? That's okay! Awareness is the first step. Next month, maybe you pack lunch twice a week and redirect that $40 toward your loan. Small shifts create big results.

My Money Goal for This Month:

"This month, I will ____
because I'm building a future where I'm free from debt and full of possibility."

Your name: ____

Month: ____

Remember: ____

You're not just budgeting—**you're designing your life**. Every conscious choice today gives you more freedom tomorrow. Keep going—you've got this!

Month ___________________________________

Monthly Take-Home Pay (After Taxes)

$ ____________________

(This is your net income—the amount that actually hits your bank account.)

Fixed Expenses *(Same amount every month)*

Category	*Budgetd Amount*	*Actual Spent*
Rent	*$*	*$*
Utilities (electric, water, internet)	*$*	*$*
Phone Bill	*$*	*$*
Student Loan Payment	*$*	*$*
Transportation (car payment, gas, transit pass)	*$*	*$*
Insurance (health, car, renters)	*$*	*$*
Subscriptions (Spotify, Netflix, etc.)	*$*	*$*
Total Fixed	*$*	*$*

Variable Expenses (*Changes each month.*)

Category	*Budgeted Amount*	*Actual Spent*
Groceries	*$*	*$*
Dining Out / Coffee	*$*	*$*
Entertainment (movies, concerts, etc.)	*$*	*$*
Shopping (clothes, gadgets, etc.)	*$*	*$*
Personal Care (haircut, toiletries)	*$*	*$*
Side Hustle Costs (if applicable)	*$*	*$*
Gifts / Donations	*$*	*$*
Total Variable	$	$

Financial Goals this Month

Category	*Amount*
Emergency Fund Savings	*$*
Extra Student Loan Payment	*$*
Retirement (e.g., 401k or Roth IRA)	*$*
Fun Money Set Aside	*$*
Total Goals	*$*

Monthly Summary

Total Income: $ ______________________________

Total Spent (Fixed + Variable): $ _____________________

Amount Left Over: $ _________________

(Income – Total Spent = What you can save, invest, or roll into next month)

Reflection: Did you spend more than planned on dining out? That's okay! Awareness is the first step. Next month, maybe you pack lunch twice a week and redirect that $40 toward your loan. Small shifts create big results.

My Money Goal for This Month:

*"This month, I will*____
because I'm building a future where I'm free from debt and full of possibility."

Your name: ____

Month: ____

Remember: ____

You're not just budgeting—**you're designing your life**. Every conscious choice today gives you more freedom tomorrow. Keep going—you've got this!

Month ______________________________

Monthly Take-Home Pay (After Taxes)

$ ________________

(This is your net income—the amount that actually hits your bank account.)

Fixed Expenses *(Same amount every month)*

Category	*Budgetd Amount*	*Actual Spent*
Rent	$	$
Utilities (electric, water, internet)	$	$
Phone Bill	$	$
Student Loan Payment	$	$
Transportation (car payment, gas, transit pass)	$	$
Insurance (health, car, renters)	$	$
Subscriptions (Spotify, Netflix, etc.)	$	$
Total Fixed	$	$

Variable Expenses (*Changes each month.*)

Category	*Budgeted Amount*	*Actual Spent*
Groceries	$	$
Dining Out / Coffee	$	$
Entertainment (movies, concerts, etc.)	$	$
Shopping (clothes, gadgets, etc.)	$	$
Personal Care (haircut, toiletries)	$	$
Side Hustle Costs (if applicable)	$	$
Gifts / Donations	$	$
Total Variable	$	$

Financial Goals this Month

Category	*Amount*
Emergency Fund Savings	*$*
Extra Student Loan Payment	*$*
Retirement (e.g., 401k or Roth IRA)	*$*
Fun Money Set Aside	*$*
Total Goals	*$*

Monthly Summary

Total Income: $ ____________________

Total Spent (Fixed + Variable): $ ______________

Amount Left Over: $ ___________

(Income – Total Spent = What you can save, invest, or roll into next month)

Reflection: Did you spend more than planned on dining out? That's okay! Awareness is the first step. Next month, maybe you pack lunch twice a week and redirect that $40 toward your loan. Small shifts create big results.

My Money Goal for This Month:

"This month, I will ____
because I'm building a future where I'm free from debt and full of possibility."

Your name: ____

Month: ____

Remember: ____

You're not just budgeting—**you're designing your life**. Every conscious choice today gives you more freedom tomorrow. Keep going—you've got this!

DEBT MOUNTAIN

Debt Payoff Strategy & Timeline Visualizer

Find Your Path. See Your Progress. Feel the Freedom.

Hey future-debt-free-you!

You've already done the hardest part: you showed up. You're tracking your loans, you know your numbers, and now you're ready to *actually pay this thing off.*

The good news? There's no single "right" way—only **the right way for YOU**. Some people need quick wins to stay motivated (hello, Debt Snowball!). Others want to save the most money long-term (that's the Debt Avalanche). And if your income is still finding its footing, an Income-Driven Plan might be your smartest move.

This page helps you **choose your strategy**—then **see exactly how long it'll take** to become debt-free. And yes, even an extra $20/month can shave months (or years!) off your timeline.

So take a breath. Grab a pen. And let's map your escape route from student debt—together.

✅ **How to Use This Section**:

- Complete at the start of your payoff journey
- Revisit every 3–6 months to update your timeline
- Celebrate every milestone—*even $1,000 paid off deserves a coffee treat!*

See you soon, gorgeous.
$1k
paid!
paid!

Freedom Views
$1k
$1k
$1k
paid!
$1k paid!
Debt-Free Mountain

Step 1: Which Strategy Fits Your Life?

Answer these quick questions to find your best path:

Quick Quiz:

- **Is your income stable and predictable?**
  [ ] Yes → Consider Standard, Avalanche, or Snowball
  [ ] No → Look into Income-Driven Repayment (IDR)

- **Do you get discouraged easily?**
  [ ] Yes → Debt Snowball (quick wins = big motivation!)
  [ ] No → Debt Avalanche (saves you the most on interest)

- **Are you working in public service (nonprofit, government, teaching)?**
  [ ] Yes → PSLF + IDR could forgive your balance in 10 years!
  [ ] No → Focus on payoff speed or affordability

- **Do you have high-interest private loans (>6%)?**
  [ ] Yes → Consider refinancing (after building credit)
  [ ] No → Stick with federal plans if eligible

Your Strategy Summary

[ ] My chosen strategy:
[ ] Standard Repayment (10 years, fixed payments)
[ ] Income-Driven Repayment (payment based on income)
[ ] Debt Snowball (pay smallest balance first)
[ ] Debt Avalanche (pay highest interest first)
[ ] PSLF Track (for public service workers)

Why I chose this:

Step 2: Payoff Timeline Visualizer

"What gets measured gets managed." — Peter Drucker

Fill in your key numbers:

- Total Student Loan Debt: $ ______________
- Average Interest Rate: __________%
- Current Monthly Payment: $ ____________
- Extra I Can Add Monthly (even $10 counts!): $_________
- New Total Monthly Payment: $__________________
  (Current + Extra)

Your Estimated Payoff Date:

Monthly Payment	*Estimated Payoff Date*	*Total Interest Paid*	*Time Saved vs. Minimum*
$ (minimum)		*$*	
$ (with extra)		*$*	*months/years*

Example:
Debt: $35,000 | Rate: 5.5% | Min Payment: $380 → Payoff in 10 years, $10,600 interest
Add $75/month → Payoff in 7 years 2 months, $2,400 less interest!

Step 3: Visual Progress Tracker

Color in one box for every $500 (or $1,000) you pay down!

1 ☐
2 ☐
3 ☐
4 ☐

Total boxes = Total Debt ÷ $500 (e.g., $30,000 = 60 boxes)

Tip: Laminate this and use a dry-erase marker—or print a new one each quarter!

My Debt-Free Vision

"I'm paying off my loans so I can..."

____

____

____

Signed,

____

Date: ______________________________

Final Encouragement:

You're not just paying off debt—you're buying back your future. Every payment is a vote for the life you want: unburdened, bold, and full of possibility. Keep going. Freedom is closer than you think.

Debt Free
Future You!

FoodDash

Side Hustle & Income Boost Tracker

Earn More. Pay Off Faster. Build Confidence.

Hey go-getter!

You're already doing the smart thing by budgeting and tracking your loans—but what if you could **speed up your payoff without cutting more from your budget?**

The secret? **Earn a little extra.**

You don't need a second full-time job. Even $50–$150/month from a side gig can knock months off your loan term and save you hundreds (or thousands!) in interest. Plus, side hustles help you build skills, expand your network, and remind you: "*I am capable of creating opportunity.*"

This page helps you brainstorm realistic gigs, track your extra income, and **watch that "extra" turn into real progress** on your debt.

Remember: Your time is valuable—but so is your freedom. Let's make both work for you.

Extra $75
= 1 month closer
to Bali?
GigWorker
Food
Order:
On the
way.
SOLD

Step 1: Side Hustle Ideas for New Grads

✅ **Low-Time, High-Flexibility**

- Tutor online (math, writing, test prep)
- Sell unused items (clothes, textbooks, gadgets)
- Participate in paid research studies or surveys
- Deliver food (DoorDash, Uber Eats – weekends only!)

✅ **Skill-Based (Leverage Your Degree!)**

- Freelance writing/editing (Upwork, Fiverr)
- Graphic design or social media management
- Resume/CV editing for fellow grads
- Virtual assistant for small businesses

✅ **Passive or Semi-Passive**

- Rent out a parking spot or spare room (if applicable)
- Create a simple digital product (printable planner, Canva template)
- Affiliate links in a niche blog or Instagram

Pro Tip: Start with one idea that fits your energy and schedule. *Even 3–5 hours/week adds up!*

Step 2: Monthly Side Income Tracker

Month	*Side Hustle Type*	*Hours Worked*	*Gross Earnings*	*Net After Fees/ Taxes*	*Amount Applied to Loans*	*Notes*
Jan			$	$	$	
Feb			$	$	$	
Mar			$	$	$	
Apr			$	$	$	
May			$	$	$	
June			$	$	$	
July			$	$	$	
August			$	$	$	
September			$	$	$	
October			$	$	$	
November			$	$	$	
December			$	$	$	

Reflection: Which hustle gave you the best return on time? Which felt most enjoyable? *Double down on that!*

Step 3: Extra Payment Impact Calculator

Every dollar you earn extra = a faster path to freedom.

Extra Monthly Income	*New Total Loan Payment*	*Estimated Time Saved*	*Interest Saved*
$25	$________	____ *months*	$________
$50	$________	____ *months*	$________
$100	$________	____ *months*	$________

Use your Loan Inventory Worksheet to estimate impact—or try the free calculator at studentaid.gov/loan-simulator

My Side Hustle Goal This Month

"This month, I will earn an extra $__________________ by______________________
so I can pay down my student loans and move closer to my dream of__________________."

My name:______________________________

Month: ______________________________

Final Thought:

You're not just earning money—you're reclaiming time. Every extra dollar shortens the years you'll spend in debt and gives you back weekends, peace of mind, and the ability to say "yes" to opportunities (not just bills).

Keep going. Your future self is already thanking you.

Tip for Use:

- Set a monthly side-income goal ($25, $50, etc.)
- Track it like a mini-business—because it is!
- Celebrate when you hit it (a $5 coffee counts as a win!)

Emergency Fund Builder

Because Life Happens—And You Deserve Peace of Mind

Hey future-you protector!

You're working hard to pay off student loans—and that's amazing. But here's a gentle truth: **if you don't have a cushion for surprises, one flat tire or dental bill could send you right back into credit card debt.**

An emergency fund isn't "extra" money—it's your **financial seatbelt.** It means when life throws a curveball (and it will!), you won't derail your debt payoff plan.

The best part? You don't need thousands overnight. Start small. Build slowly. Every $5, $10, or $20 you tuck away is a vote for your future self's calm, confidence, and control.

This page helps you build your safety net—step by step—without guilt, overwhelm, or perfectionism. Because freedom isn't just about paying off debt it's about sleeping well at night.

$500

"This isn't boring—it's your peace of mind in glitter."

Step 1: Your 3-Phase Emergency Fund Plan

Phase	*Goal*	*Why It Matters*	*Where to Keep It*
1. Mini Fund	*$500*	*Covers small emergencies (e.g., phone repair, urgent prescription)*	*High-yield savings account (HYSA) or regular savings*
2. Essentials Buffer	*1 month of essential expenses (rent, food, loan payment, utilities)*	*Protects you if you lose income temporarily*	*Separate savings account (not checking!)*
3. Full Safety Net	*3–6 months of essentials*	*True peace of mind for job loss, medical issues, etc.*	*HYSA or money market account*

Essential Expenses Example:

Rent ($900) + Groceries ($250) + Loan Payment ($200) + Utilities ($100) = $1,450/month
→ Phase 2 goal = $1,450

Step 2: Monthly Savings Tracker

Month	*Amount Saved This Month*	*Total Saved So Far*	*Phase Reached? (✓)*
January	$	$	☐ Mini ($500)
February	$	$	☐ Essentials
March	$	$	☐ Full Safety Net
April	$	$	
May	$	$	
June	$	$	
July	$	$	
August	$	$	
September	$	$	
October	$	$	
November	$	$	
December	$	$	

Tip: Set up an automatic transfer on payday—*even $10/week adds up to $520/year*!

Step 3: Where to Find "Extra" for Your Fund

You don't need a raise—just a few smart shifts:

- **Round up** your debit card purchases (use apps like Acorns or your bank's roundup feature)
- **Pause one subscription** for a month (streaming, gym, app) → redirect that $15
- **Sell 3 things** you don't use (Facebook Marketplace, Poshmark, OfferUp)
- **Put windfalls here first**: tax refunds, birthday cash, work bonuses

✅ **Remember**: This money **is off-limits**—except for true emergencies (not sales, vacations, or "I really want this" moments).

✅ My Emergency Fund Intention

"I'm building my emergency fund so I never have to choose between my student loan payment and a car repair again.

My goal this month is to save $ ______________ *by* ______________________________."

My name: ______________________________

Month: ______________________________

Final Encouragement:

An emergency fund isn't about fear—**it's about freedom**. It's the quiet confidence that says, "*I've got this—no matter what.*"

You're not just saving money. You're building resilience. And that's priceless.

Keep going. You're doing better than you think.

✅ **How to Use This Page:**

- Print and fill out at the start of each month
- Celebrate every $100 milestone (yes, really!)
- Once you hit Phase 1, treat yourself to a small joy—*with cash you already budgeted!*

CREDIT SCORE:
520

Credit Score & Financial Health Check

Plus: Your Future You Vision Board

Hey dreamer-doer!

You're paying off loans, building savings, and tracking every dollar like a pro. Now let's talk about something powerful but often overlooked: **your credit score**.

This three-digit number might feel mysterious—but it's actually your **financial reputation**. A strong score means better interest rates on cars, apartments, and even insurance. It can help you rent your first place, land a job (yes, some employers check!), and one day buy a home.

And while we're at it—let's not forget **why** you're doing all this hard work. That's where your **Future You** comes in: the version of you who's debt-free, confident, and living life on your own terms.

This page helps you **check your financial health today**—and **connect it to the life you're building tomorrow**. Because you're not just managing money... you're designing your future.

Debt-free by 28!
First solo trip
"My credit score is my love language"

Don't Get Discouraged! Low Credit Scores Can Be Raised.

PS: Still eating
ramen sometimes.
It's fine.

Step 1: Credit Score Quick Check

What's Your Score? *(Check for free!)*

- **Free sources:** AnnualCreditReport.com, Credit Karma, Experian, or your bank/credit card app
- **My current score:** ____________________
- **Date checked:** ______________________

What's a "good" score?

- 670–739 = Good
- 740–799 = Very Good
- 800+ = Excellent
  (Don't panic if you're below 670—you're just getting started!)

Step 2: Financial Health Checklist

Place a ✓ next to each habit you've started—or want to start!

[ ] I know my credit score and check it quarterly

[ ] I pay all bills on time (even $5 subscriptions!)

[ ] I keep credit card balances below 30% of my limit

[ ] I have at least one credit card (used lightly and paid in full)

[ ] I've reviewed my credit report for errors (annualcreditreport.com)

[ ] I avoid opening too many new accounts at once

[ ] I've set up autopay for at least one bill to avoid late fees

[ ] I understand how student loans affect my credit (on-time payments = good!)

Fun fact: Just **one late student loan payment** can drop your score by 50–100 points. But consistent on-time payments? They build your score like bricks in a foundation.

Step 3: Quick Wins to Boost Your Score

Action	*Impact*	*Timeline*
Set up autopay for loans & cards	*Prevents late payments*	*Immediate*
Pay down credit card balance to <30%	*Lowers credit utilization*	*1 billing cycle*
Keep old credit card open (even if unused)	*Lengthens credit history*	*Long-term*
Dispute errors on credit report	*Fixes unfair dings*	*30–60 days*

Be kind to yourself: Building credit is a marathon—not a sprint. Every responsible choice counts.

Step 4: Future You Vision Board

"I'm doing this so I can ____"

Close your eyes for a moment. Imagine your life **2–5 years from now**, after your student loans are paid off. What does it look like?

- Where are you living?
- What are you doing for work—or joy?
- How do you feel when you check your bank account?
- What freedom do you now have that you don't today?

Now, write or sketch it below. Use words, doodles, magazine cutouts (if printing), or just describe it with your heart.

My Future Self Letter

Dear Future Me,

Right now, I'm working hard, budgeting carefully, and saying "no" to things so I can say "YES" to you.

I hope you're... ______________________________

____

____

____

I hope you've traveled to ______________________________

I hope you wake up feeling ______________________________

Most of all, I hope you know: **I believed in you enough to start today.**

With love,
Your Present Self

Name: ______________________________

Date: ____________________

One Small Step Toward That Future

This week, I will: ______________________________

____

____

(e.g., "Check my credit report," "Set up autopay," "Open a high-yield savings account")

Final Thought:

Your credit score is a tool. Your vision is your compass. Together, they guide you toward a life that's not just financially stable—but deeply fulfilling.

You're not just building credit.

You're building **a life you love.**

Keep going. Future You is already proud of you.

✅ **How to Use This Page:**

- Complete the checklist monthly
- Re-read your "Future You" letter whenever motivation dips
- Tape this page to your wall or keep it in your planner as a reminder

Congratulations!

You now have 6 core worksheets for your Post-Grad Financial Planner:

1. Loan Inventory
2. Income & Expense Tracker
3. Debt Payoff Strategy & Timeline
4. Side Hustle & Income Boost Tracker
5. Emergency Fund Builder
6. Credit Score + Future You Vision

CREDIT SCORE:
825

Remember,
You Got
This!

Made in the USA
Monee, IL
02 November 2026

67383845R00072